When Love Was Reels

Poetry

When Love Was Reels

Poetry

José B. González

Arte Público Press
Houston, Texas

When Love Was Reels: Poetry is funded in part by a grant from the City of Houston through the Houston Arts Alliance. We are grateful for their support.

Recovering the past, creating the future

Arte Público Press
University of Houston
4902 Gulf Fwy, Bldg 19, Rm 100
Houston, Texas 77204-2004

Cover photo by José B. González
Cover design by Victoria Castillo

Names: González, José B. author.
Title: When love was reels : poetry / by José B. González.
Description: Houston, TX : Arte Público Press, 2017.
Identifiers: LCCN 2017027699| ISBN 9781558858503 (alk. paper) | ISBN 9781518504358 (kindle) | ISBN 9781518504365 (pdf)
Classification: LCC PS3607.O56185 A6 2017 | DDC 811/.6—dc23
LC record available at https://lccn.loc.gov/2017027699

∞ The paper used in this publication meets the requirements of the American National Standard for Information Sciences—Permanence of Paper for Printed Library Materials, ANSI Z39.48-1984.

Printed in the United States of America

17 18 19 20 5 4 3 2 1

Table of Contents

Acknowledgments

I'm grateful to Arte Público Press for being willing to allow me to be a part of its impressive history of giving Latino authors a voice. In particular, I'd like to thank Dr. Nicolás Kanellos and Gabriela Baeza Ventura, for their skilled eyes, and Marina Tristán, whose encouraging kindness gave me faith. My Mamá Noy and my Tío Alfredo served as inspiration for this book. They, along with my sister, Evelyn, my brother, Ivan, and Tía Reina, were with me at various times as we watched characters come to life on the big screen. Many of the actors and filmmakers mentioned in this book faced their own, very real challenges. Without their perseverance, this work would not be possible. My wife, Kristin, was very helpful by giving me thumbs up or down during the revision process. My girls, Cassandra, Olivia and Sofia, allowed me writing time by being great students, while my son, Nolan, has given me enough motivation and material to write bulky novels.

The following poems or versions of the poems were originally published in:

"Scene from The Ballad of Gregorio Cortez." *Codex Journal.* 25 June 2015.

"Scene with Dolores del Río," and "Scene from *Los Olvidados*." *Theatre Under My Skin: Contemporary Salvadoran Poetry*. San Salvador: Kalina Press, 2014.

"Scene from *Walk Proud* (1979)" and "Scene with Marcelino Sánchez: *The Warriors* (1979)." *Kweli Journal*. Summer, 2016.

"Scene with Ricardo Montalbán, *Fantasy Island* (1977–1984)." *Pittsburgh Poetry Review*. Fall, 2016.

"Scene with Tin Tan: *El rey del barrio* (1949)." *Revista ARS.* Número 10, 2016.

"Scene with Pancho: *The Cisco Kid* (1950-1956)." *The Wandering Song: Central American Writing in the United States.* Tia Chucha, 2017.

Dedication

To the actors who played the part and kept me company while my family was apart.

SCENES FROM THE GOLDEN ERA

Scene from *Los olvidados* (1950)

Forgotten (children)

My grandmother tightens her hands
around mine when the gang of children robs
a blind man. Forgotten children. To forget
is to leave a pencil behind, to leave
a house door open, to leave a light
on inside a house. Forgotten are names,
numbers. They are accidents of the mind.

My parents crossed when I started losing
teeth. My memory of them is broken, chipped
away. Neighbors used to tell me that they
would come back with a bicycle, that
they would ride back from a northern sky.

Then the talk of returning stopped. The wheel
never made a circle. My head turns away
from the screen. The children who steal
who beg who cheat who punch back who
lie who loot who pilfer who plunder who
pirate who poach who leave the lights
on do not forget. I whisper to myself,
They. I. Will not be forgotten. I. They.
Will not be (forgotten) children.

Scene from *Los paquetes de Paquita* (1955)

There is a girl, Mena, in my class.

Her face is on the screen: Paquita.

Hair: waves of the Pacific.

Eyes: color of a cool night.

Eyelashes: curbs of a moon.

Lips: a morning on the Pacific
                    sipping chocolate
                              lying on a hammock.

Paquita is on a river, at a wedding
on a boat, with men in suits, women
in their silks. A woman crashes
the celebration on a canoe.

Paquita grabs then rides the hair
of the woman, sinking the woman
into a river. Even men can't hold
Paquita's arms back.

I've seen Mena fight too. The play-
ground behind the school. A girl
who wears skirts and carries Bibles
clawed Mena on her arm, a scratch
that looked like a dirty river. Mena
pulls her hair and won't end
the tug of war, she swears to hold

on until the creeks dry. Girls
cover their mouths, boys howl
and pat each other on the back.

Where we live, the babies'
fists start to fly in the womb,
some aim for the cord, others
for the abdomen. They all break
water with the force of animals
stuck inside traps. Once they see
light, they have to choose sides.

Drinking tainted milk, some choose
hate. Others choose love of hate. I
choose waves, the Pacific, chocolate,
a hammock. Mena.

Scene from *Nosotros los pobres* (1948)

La Chachita asks her father to paint a memory of her mother's braids, to tell her where they are buried. Oh father, what have you done to her? You killed her. You killed her. But a father can't take those words, so he slaps her, then punches, bloodies the wall.

As the scene ends, Chachita hugs him, forgiving him, forgiving herself, even as her teeth are masked by spurts of blood. Before the scene ends, my grandmother is crying, crawling into my pupils, wondering why they're not releasing a flood.

When the brave cry, they remember volcanoes. My grandmother expects me to ask about my ______ 's breath but when a tree starts dropping leaves, the tree is barely a tree. My ______ is gone. She and my _________ left me, and I shouldn't call her my ______.

I could pluck wilted memories of the days when she wore an apron around the house. Ask about how my _______ met _____ or what they wore at their wedding. But when a ______ starts to drop its leaves, the ______ is no longer a _____.

The father in the film loves the child. That's why he stays. And he loves La Chorreada, Blanca Estela Pavón, a woman with wavy hair and eyes so soft they could launch the types of revolutions that would make _______ stay at home with their children.

My grandmother tells me that in real life, Blanca died when she was 23, the same age as my ______ when ______ left. In real life, Blanca's plane crashed near a volcano in Mexico. In real life, she continues. In real life, maybe my _________ is near that volcano.

I don't ask, but my grandmother tells me more. Blanca's last film was *La mujer que yo perdí*. Her eyes tear up as she tells me the title. *The Woman that I Lost*. Not mine. Not even a drop. She adds more about Pedro Infante. I stare hard at the screen.

How he loved airplanes. How he too died in a plane crash. They identified his body among the remains by the bracelet bearing his name. Her crying gets heavier. Twenty years later, some people think that he still walks among us. That he has breath.

She finally asks me why I don't cry. But I just stare at La Chorreada and Pedro Infante as they hold hands with locked eyes. She tells me that they were also together in other movies, like *Cuando lloran los valientes (When the Courageous Cry)*.

Films help my grandmother, the courageous one, remember the truth. But I use their light to forget. Each time Pedro and La Chorreada kiss, the screen tells a lie that lives and grows. As the projector rolls, I can feel my _______s' breath, forget their ________.

Scene with Capulina: *La sombra del otro* (1957)

He wears his sports jacket snuggled
against his shoulders, cap tilted
like a jester's crown, the king of falling.
His sleeves don't reach his wrists,
and when he walks, the screen shakes.

I have seen him fly planes
and wrestle mummies, raise
babies with moustaches and even
kick a saint. But when Capulina
sings, "La aventura," with Viruta
at his side, serenading two women,
I almost leave him at the cinema,
stretching my hand away from
my grandmother's.

The women's lips rest on Capulina
but he can't leap beyond the first few
lyrics, his crying stuck in his throat, his
guitar sputtering, remembering
silent moments of his love life.

His explanation: the song is too sad.

Capulina restarts and restarts
the refrain, but the song keeps falling
back on fragments of the past. Viruta
stones him with stares, tells him to be
macho (like the singers with cowboy
hats). A man crying like that in front
of a woman. It's enough for me
to walk away.

But just as I am about to go through
the exit doors, Capulina swallows
sorrow, finishes the song, his feet
wiggling back and forth in celebration,
as if to prove he is still a man.

To play the guitar, cry in front
of a girl and dance. To wear
clothes that don't fit. To toss
memories into the ground after
they've stripped your voice.

To love Mena, the only girl
in the class who whispers
a smile when our eyes lock,
the only one whose eyes shouted
over giggles when I shut my lids
to stop the flow of a flood
in front of our fifth-grade class
on Father's Day when Oscar Ríos
sang verses about how he found
a rusty hammer on the side
of the road, how he called it Papi.

To wish guitar strings on my fingers,
a girl like Mena in my arms, the drum
of a hammer in my sleep, to forget
in order to sing. To be Capulina.

Scene with Tin Tan: *El rey del barrio* (1949)

On the way to school, I pace
ahead of my grandmother, as I
kick
the
cans
that litter the streets.

Today I'd rather be Tin
Tan.

Tin Tan's lips have touched more
women than any other screen star.

I have seen him kiss the curves
that turn and slap him,
sometimes they laugh at him.

He moves his mouth like he's
fi-ring
a pistol and he wears
baggy pants
that
dance
by
themselves

(Like the ones my grandmother
makes me wear. Two sizes
too much to overcome.)

Words are his bullets, and
his mouth curves toward

the sunset. When he
talks, his

          teeth

                      stick out

(like mine).

Even when beaten
                                dizzy,
Tin Tan can turn
from a boxer who gets punched
by a tiny man to the weapon
that
          can.

He steals from the
rich
     and escapes from jails.

Tin Tan.
                    He can.

Walking to school, I curl
                                        my lips
and reload
                                        my mouth,
ready to take on the boys
who toss fire
                                 at me
(for being me).

They make
my eyes swell and they pull
petals from the wild-
flowers
I want to deliver to
Mena.

Today, as I walk into school,
I will show everyone
the teeth inside my smile.
I will stand in front of Mena, open my pockets,
give her the candies I stole from Don Moncho's
store and fire words of love.

I can.

Scene with Dolores del Río: *Bird of Paradise* (1932)

From the river. Sorrows
flow, begin with a sacrifice,
Dolores. Her face catches
an islander's eyes. And in turn,
a tall, fair-skinned Tarzan catches
hers. A ring of fire surrounds her,
he Tarzan, she Sorrow. Her hands,
bird wings flutter around her body,
half-naked, a lei covering her breasts.

Hips to the gods. The tribe follows
her moves, a sway, a way of saying
seduction. They worship with drums,
raise their spears above her head.

The Islander, convinced that her spirit
has entered him, dances with his head
down, rapture of capture. But Tarzan
scoops, carries her to a boat, away
from the maddening Indians.

So much of Mena, whose hair
waves are full of sand, her house
near the beach. If I could, I
would rescue Mena from stains
on her blouse, carry her
on my shoulders, away
from our class, down

the hall and into a room
where skin wouldn't wrinkle,
teeth wouldn't fall, and sorrow
would only be a name.

But I am me. More Indian
than Tarzan.

Scene from *Los bandidos del Río Frío* (1938)

A villain's hero. Scraggly beard/facial hair,
he wears a grin on his face/eyes
and gets the movie reel seething/speeding,
the music rising over a mountain/hill.

A purse in the hands of a widow/dying lover,
containing a family's life/savings,
disappears from the grave/cemetery
as the Bandido takes all/nothing.

On a pale horse, the Bandido escapes/returns
with a laughter that trots toward sunsets/sunrises,
his hard laugh the proof of his crimes/guilt,
echoing loudly in towns' bars/banks.

Sundays when my grandmother boils/cooks
a soup for her afternoon nap, I chase/capture
the Bandido before the hero shoots/kills
him. Seven days later, he is reborn/resuscitated.

I play the Bandido at candy stores/stands,
pull my fingers' triggers and take/pocket
rockets, pops, gumballs and walk/escape
with my head down through streets/alleys.

So much/so little of him makes me remember/forget
the beginnings/ends of so many movies/films
when a bad guy/bandido steals for kicks/laughs
as if his father/mother had left him behind/alone.

The audience will clap/cheer as the Bandido falls/dies
with his face/body on the ground/earth
but without his grin/gun, the hero cannot be born/return.
So I pull for my Bandido/hero to rise/stand.

He's all I have. All I am is a boy/man.

Scene with Sara García: *Dueña y señora* (1948)

The screen: an apron, the size of a table full of bottles of aged wine and fine china.

Action: The gray-haired maid yells about pepper, food spills, a broken carburetor and short blouses. She serves food with a toss of the wrist. Hawking around the table, she hears the family talking about the new wife who will be sleeping in the house, on the old bed, the one the mother slept on. Her arms akimbo, she demands with a nod and commands with a curl of the lip.

My Grandmother's Reaction: She laughs at the maid's arms, the way she picks up shards with a snarl and places her ears outside bedroom doors, leaps into private conversations, uses her chin to stare at others, combs her hair in obedient streaks, carries her voice through oak doors in every room and walks as if her coins had bought the floors she scrubs.

My Reaction: I stare at the maid's posture, the way she moves with her shoulders high into the heavens, stands straight like the board on which she irons the family's clothes. I'd like to see my grandmother walk tall too but she drags each leg like a broken broom, and her shoulders are heavy, like a stack of irons. Each time she brings coins home, she carries them with two hands and drops them at my feet. At night, she prays with rosary beads. When I go to sleep, I imagine her ordering gods to follow her orders. I imagine her when she could stand straight. I imagine her yelling at her son to make his bed, to get his elbows off the table, to walk like a man. I imagine her telling him to wake up. I imagine her watching him grow taller than her. I imagine her warning him not to risk the trip across volcanoes and deserts. I imagine her back breaking as she fights him to stay home. I imagine her arms being stronger than the hungry promises of dreams.

Scene with Cantinflas: *Ahí está el detalle* (1940)

Ahí está el detalle. The details. Like picking small rocks out of a pile of beans. A small detail can make a difference between hopping on a bus and getting killed by a bus.

Picture a dog, no collar, wandering the streets. It wants a bone. A turkey leg, a greasy rib, a lamb chop. It doesn't know the difference. Could be a dinosaur bone, a chicken bone. It's hungry. So hungry it could swallow whole bones and choke on any bite.

Picture a dog barking. Begging for a bite of a bread crumb. It wanders. Scurries from side to side, door to door, street to street, town to town. It chases pigeons, butterflies, lizards, cars. It's been chased side to side from doors, from streets, from towns.

Picture a hot day. Sweat on your forehead trickling to your ankles. Sweat weighing your feet down. The sweltering concrete pulling you toward a flame. Your head is bowed down, your arms are at your sides, ready to surrender to the sun's scorching rays.

Picture your grandmother next to you, holding her purse to her side with both hands. She is on a street full of traffic, full of loud horns. Beggars and bottles are on the sidewalk. She tells you not to stop at the coo of each pigeon. That you're going to miss the bus.

Picture the dog again shifting between cars and buses, dodging. That dog. Remember? The one that was chasing pigeons, butterflies, lizards, cars? The one with the spot on its nose. The one without a collar, wandering the streets. That one. It's still hungry. And it's still wandering. It's limping a little as it nears the bus. Your bus. The dog snarls a little at the back tire, but on a hot day, when you've been chasing pigeons, butterflies, lizards and cars, wouldn't you do the same? The dog puts its head down, the way an obedient dog would after a snarl. Your grandmother looks back, smiling that you didn't miss the bus, but shaking her head because you still haven't caught up. You move past the back tire. And at that moment. No, actually, at the moment that you remember the film. How Cantinflas' girlfriend asked him to kill the dog. Because it was rabid. How he refused at first. But she begged. So he took a gun, closed his eyes and fired. Cantinflas shot it. Killed it. That Cantinflas. And no barks or laughter. Now come back to the street. The one with beggars and bottles on sidewalks. The one with the dog without a leash.

Picture that dog snarling again. Except this time, the dog sneaks up behind the back tire. You run at the same instant that he lunges in your direction. The dog looks taller up close, its head up to your chest, a breath away. The spot on its nose the size of your head.

Picture the dog's bite on your leg. Little red dots .... around your calf .... A man wearing a blue bandana kicks the dog in the stomach. Someone says something about not touching the dog. It is drooling. It may have rabies. The dog sprints, leaping between cars and buses. Your grandmother grabs your hand. Stares at the little red dots .... The bus exhales black smoke into the sidewalk. You don't scream because you've been taught that big boys don't cry. But you whimper. Because it's not just a few dots .... The dog was hungry. Remember? It wanted a bone. A turkey leg, a greasy rib, a lamb chop. It found a bone. Your left calf.

Picture two weeks later. The rabies shots on your stomach .... Your bite wounds haven't healed .... Your grandmother is taking you home from the last shot. She makes sure you're at her side before getting on the bus home. As you board it, you look at the back tire to make sure no dogs are hiding on the other side. On the way home, you go back through the same streets. The ones with beggars and bottles on sidewalks. You see the dogs without leashes. You notice that they all look like the dog that bit you. You see the wounds on the streets ———. Then you recall the dog's snarl as it was about to bite you. You recall the sharpness of the teeth. The dive of the snout. The rise of the ears. Then that detail that no one else could see. But you. The teats on the dog's underside ::::

Picture the memory: :::: a mother, the streets ———, the details of rabid hunger ....

Scene with Lupe Vélez: *Hollywood Party* (1934)

her dress,
a flower full
of teatime
petals,

but the thorns
in her mouth
jab and stab.

she doesn't
bother to cross
her legs, lone
woman
at the bar.

her heels
poke back
at the fat
and the skinny
of the men.

she starts
with the shell
of an egg,
the yolk
that winds up
on the sequins
of her dress,

she smirks
then slaps
Laurel, then
punches

Hardy in
the gut.

Lupe is why
I shy away
from Mena.

as I limp
into class,
Mena's eyes
don't whisper
sorry
for the dog bites,
(or the shots),
they don't
even turn
from the sun
to face
the drag
of my foot-
steps.

I wish I
could tell
her my wounds
were for her
lips, that I ran
over volcanoes
and jumped
on dog's teeth
for a chance
to be, for us
to become, but
Mena has Lupe
in her blood
and I have

a fat wound
that won't
stop seeping
and a skinny
wrist too weak
to carry orchids
to her feet. instead,
I bring her candies
and wait for her
lips to sweeten,
stop inhaling
Lupe's fire,
start exhaling
the bliss
of that first
kiss.

Scene from *María Candelaria* (1943)

The painting is simple like nudity. Like
putting on a wedding dress. Like

painting a breast. Like
stripping off a dress. Like

hearing my grandmother say
María is like Mena's mother. Like

hearing her say those women drink
to the tides of the dark. Like

hearing her say that they sleep
when the moon's men awaken. Like

hearing Mena's neighbor say it's true,
the doors are unlocked at night. Like

putting a note on Mena's desk to say
I would like to walk her home. Like

hearing her whisper come with me
and tasting a drop of her smile. Like

holding her hand so tight our secrets
could never be released into the wind.

Scene from *¡Vámonos con Pancho Villa!* (1936)

A fly on a pear on a box
on a stand on a road
near a peasant who backs
slowly away from
the man with a gun.

The man with two friends
looking for something
to do, a dance or a drink,
or a woman to meet,
aims toward a head.

He fires one time
and shows off the hole
on the pear from the shot
and laughs with his friends
over the death of a fly.

They walk away, pear
in their hands, without
paying a cent for taking
the fruit of a man
just manning his stand.

On a shelf at a market
near my grandmother's
home, at a stand that sells
candy and gum, I eye
sweets on a shelf.

I don't have a gun,
don't laugh with a grin,

don't walk with friends,
don't bother to pay,
I take what I can.

A man grabs my arm,
kicks me on the rear.
As I fall on the dirt
flat on my chest,
I can't take a breath.

Later, they won't ask
why, they won't hear
the buzz, they'll just
swat at my head,
and toss me aside.

They'll forget I'm a fly
on a pear on a box
on a stand on a road
on a land that digs holes
each time a fly is born.

Scene from *Él* (1953)

1. It begins at the mass of high heels, with priests clasping hands and bowing their heads.

2. It continues with the chanting of monks that bless the water that will be used to wash feet while the high heels sneak under a pew.

3. She wears a lace mantilla and crosses herself away from his glance.

4. As he leaves church and follows her for the rest of time, he finds a new religion.

5. But she says no. Her arms are locked with another man's.

6. He wouldn't give up, even if she was going to marry his friend.

7. When she finally says yes, it's with a musical kiss.

8. They marry. Off-screen.

9. And suddenly, she's telling another man about how the marriage ended before it started.

For me,

1. It began with Mena's bare feet shuffling around the playground with teachers patrolling the rough elbows of boys.

2. It continued with the cries and yells of running and tagging, the dirty feet of children chasing each other, her feet so close to mine.

3. She wore a striped shirt that was scented with vanilla ice cream and love.

4. As she left the playground, I followed her for the rest of my country time. At night, I kneeled for the chance to see her.

5. But she said no by having her back facing me.

6. I couldn't stop chasing the sounds of her steps.

7. When she finally said yes, her lips pursed into a candy smile.

8. Not even my mother or her grandmother knew how we held hands.

9. And suddenly, when my grandmother told me that I'd be leaving to the U.S., I knew that leaving would mean finding a new god.

Scene from *Historia de un gran amor* (1942)

I only kissed her once.

Twice if we count the whisper in her
ear that crawled to her cheekbones.

During recess, while other kids
are chewing and popping gum,
I tell her about leaving.

I don't say I'll be back.

That Sunday's film is about heroes
on horseback returning home. Manuel
leaves Soledad when they still
believe in making promises. He
grows up believing in keeping
them. She believes in wedding
rings. And when he comes back
for her, nothing is the same.

Mena and I stopped worshipping
promises when we learned to walk.
But we both believe in heaven
and hell. And now the end
of beginnings and the beginnings
of ends.

I hug her without making promises
of horses and rings. And when she
finishes the goodbye candy I've
brought for her and then tosses

the wrapper on the ground as she
walks away for the last time, I
watch the wrapper float back
and forth as if it's swinging
and fighting to be held before its
beginning and end are forgotten.

Scene with Cantinflas: *El portero* (1950)

As opening credits roll,
Cantinflas sweeps the sidewalk,
tossing garbage into the wind.

His whiskered moustache fills
the screen as he drums choruses
of riddles onto a typewriter.

Our final time at the theater,
my grandmother's eyes
are closer to reaching the sky.

I weave in and out of images
of Cantinflas riding
a horse to a wreath.

He carries a bouquet of flowers
to a woman who has read
deeply into his palms.

She stares in love but brushes
past him and dives into
the arms of a man in uniform.

With bloodshot eyes, Cantinflas
types a goodbye letter, telling
her that he never loved her.

In a few months, I will be
in New York, where screens
will not be black and white.

The words coming out
of actors' mouths will
make all films silent.

I will live with my uncle,
who will let me stay home
and be the sultan of TV.

He will buy me a stack
of papers that I'll use to draw
spaceship sombreros.

After scenes fade,
I'll write letters
to my grandmother.

My hands will be sorry
for turning away from
her brittle warnings.

I will tell her how the closing
credits of films remind me
of Cantinflas scenes.

I won't tell her how
I swallow my screams,
how I watch alone.

After the screen turns black,
I'll sketch candy wrappers
and stack them like reels.

I will sign the letters
Love.

El fin.

SCENES FROM EL NORTE

Scene with Pancho: *The Cisco Kid* (1950–1956)

The first year with my uncle my belly starts to flatten. He says it's because New York water is cleaner. He doesn't let me talk much about my grandmother and tells me that I need to bury my country.

I tried to bring up the times that she and I went to movies, but he usually stops me by the time I start to mention a scene. Bury it, he says.

He never had his own kids, but that's good. For me anyway. He leaves me alone in the apartment and doesn't worry about me crossing streets, the way my grandmother did.

I thought of asking him about my ________. What ________ was like growing up. I want to know if my ________ met my ________ when they were in second grade. But my uncle keeps saying to bury it. So I stay quiet.

He has this small TV in the living room, where I sleep. He doesn't watch it much but he tells me that I need to watch as much as I can so that I can learn English. That's what he did, he says. That and burying, I bet.

There is only one Spanish channel, and that one is fuzzy most of the time. Playing with the antenna does nothing. So I have no choice but to watch TV in English anyway.

One channel plays the same show over and over. It's about two cowboys, Cisco and Pancho, who ride their horses across deserts and fight outlaws. They both have accents that don't sound like my uncle's.

Pancho's English sounds like it's for laughs, but there are no laugh tracks. He speaks in short lines and does what the Cisco Kid tells him. The time he gets kidnapped, Cisco scolds him, "Be quiet, Pancho."

I know those words from teachers at school. "Be quiet." By the end of the show, Cisco fistfights the outlaw while Pancho points a gun at a woman. The episode ends with the two of them riding free.

Each time I watch an episode, I wait for their families to show up. But they never do.

By the end of the year, I can understand most of the jokes that Pancho makes. And I can tell that they never mention their families. Not Cisco's. Not Pancho's. It's like they don't exist. Like they had to bury every part of them in order to ride into new sunsets.

Scene from Geography Lesson: *El Chavo del Ocho* (1973–1980)

Chavo's Class: Is like my old class, where students' shoes were made of faded leather scratched by the edges of jagged sidewalks. Except Chavo's class has kids with caps the color of nations' flags, girls with dirty freckles and dresses with ruffles, bowlegged boys who answer questions about stars by pointing to volcanoes. Their fingers point to name-less continents. Posters around the room show the insides of hearts, the roots of trees, and a jack-in-the-box with hands wide like Africa, Antarctica, Asia, Australia, Europe, South America and North America, my new home.

Home: Is what used to be. When the air begins to smell like gasoline or the ground begins to feel like it's on fire, I want to be in Chavo's class, tossing food and erasers, pulling chairs and skipping steps, painting the blackboard, lunging wildly at girls who carry dolls slugging late to class, lounging on my seat with my hand raised for a wrong answer, dropping to the floor to smash a spider. The teacher would aim sticks of chalk at me, and I would raise my hand to name all the continents, point to New York on the map and tell the class that this is where children sleep on sofas and dreams live in suitcases.

Scene with *Chico and the Man* (1974–1978), Part I

below the apartment's fire escape, the smell of fried
plantain rises slowly from an open window.

a rusted, empty propane tank has lost its hiss,
a stray cat has found a scrap of yesterday.

lifting its paws, heavy boots over drifts, he sifts,
then sits in a shade, sits and waits for the fall

of a feather on weathered spruce needles. he meows
loudly, shakes his tail and shifts. in a room with cracked

paint, I wear my coat and a blanket, shuffling between
plaster walls, waiting for my uncle to come home.

a far-off bell rings, but all I hear is the window's
howls and hisses. he's been gone since the sleet

turned to mix. he was out hunting chicken bones
and then got stuck on a greasy, late shift. the screen

on a crate flashes images of L.A., Boyle Heights
and summer short sleeves. a man sings, chico

and the man, to the beat of drums and guitar strings.
the words come in pieces, but I can tell that

laughter follows the old man's slurred words. on our
sixth floor an old man wears camouflage, grunts

and points to flags. my uncle tells me to stay away,
that he carries black and white photos of the way

it used to be, the times when restaurants on the street
only served pasta. he leaves trails of stares when he walks

by, carrying his grocery bags. even in winter, the old man's
midnight words fall through the floors. I catch them

as if my name is chico. my uncle says to keep the slurred
words locked, not to send them back, that this is New York,

to stay away. on tv the laughs rise when the old man tells
chico something about leaving with his flies. if I could,

I would be a robber fly, wings taking me to the sixth floor,
me with antenna and a bristled moustache. my wings

would be so fast that they would make the sound of guitars,
my legs would land so hard that they would sound like

drums and somewhere, some old man would sing, chico
chico, chico is a man. chico is a man. somewhere some

old man would save chico. a man.

Scene with *Chico and the Man* (1974–1978), Part II

at school, they call chico a junkie. pablo
ramírez says the same thing happened to

his own uncle, body found near central
park. seemed everyone knows somebody

strung out on hazy dreams. in the middle
of science class, we start singing

the theme song and instead of slamming
the music, Mr. Videll tells us about how

the same guy, José Feliciano, also sang
the National Anthem in the 1968 World

Series. Pablo responds anotherpuerto
ricanbeltingthemtunes, fist of pride

in the air. and when Mr. Videll tells us
that Feliciano was blacklisted for years

for singing about rockets glaring,
Pablo lowers his fist and sings,

don'tbediscouraged, thepuertorican-
man, heain'tsohardtounderstand.

don'tbediscouraged, thepuertorican-
man, heain'tsohardtounderstand.

Scene with Juan Epstein: *Welcome Back Kotter* (1975–1979)

Brooklyn: a city so large, apartments are piled like boxes. My uncle and I climb down from the fifth, skimming past the moldy walls on the third floor. He walks with me to a school where students fire a shotgun Spanish. They are islanders, they say, like Epstein.

Toughest kid in school, Epstein bobs his head like Groucho Marx, except he doesn't smoke cigars. He wears a pair of worn jeans and a denim jacket torn at the sleeves. His walk is almost a dance, the classroom is his boxing ring. Students know his afro.

On my second day at P.S. 181, the Epstein in second period, bandana swagger at the side of his pants, tosses a pencil at my head, yells at me. Forwalkingtooclosetohim. He tells me don't stare at him either. And that from now on, to call him by his name. Epstein.

In the show, the punches come after jokes. Here, the jokes come after punches. My hand learns to cover my face and my head learns to bob, answering to tosses and sudden swings before a fist rises. As I walk around, I listen closely for the sound of bells.

My uncle juggles jobs and girlfriends. He doesn't have the balance for three and doesn't put a leash around my neck. I'm more like a stray and can hear whistles of trains blocks away. I don't bother to give him ringside commentary about the fights at school.

On school walls, lovers and gangsters use spray cans like dog piss to mark territories. I cross borders each time I step out of the apartment. The neighbor on the 2nd reminds me to keepgoingboy when I walk by. Anytime I move, I keep my eyes on my feet.

In the show's opening credits, the path to and from school flashes on my uncle's TV. T-shirts hang on clotheslines, crowds walk inside markets. Subway cabs carry loads of graffiti. The underbelly a bridge with its streets and sidewalks takes over the screen.

A voice sings something about being back to a place with broken land. I don't understand all the words, but the tone is so familiar that I can close my eyes, hum every note and feel the guitar strings miss a place that someone somewhere sitting alone calls home.

Scene from WWF Championship Wrestling (1972–1986)

This kid in school, Pablo, wears his hair past his shoulders. Star of the football team, he dodges falls so he can spring at the snap of a finger. His nickname is Midnight Train because no one stops his tracks. He moved from Yonkers a few years back because his family wanted to dodge the Son of Sam, even after he was caught.

This WWF wrestler, Merced Solís, jumps off ropes, elbows first, tags his partner, Ivan Putski, in and out of the ring. Together, they pin the Valiant Brothers, start flashing a belt. He goes by the name Tito Santana, and he has these arm-drag moves and drop kicks that move the TV screen. His head scissors fly from corner to corner.

This teacher, Mr. Almeida, carries this briefcase the size of the Empire State Building. He dodges these spitballs and uses his chalk as a shield. His nickname is Mr. Fly, because he has a swatter in his desk that he uses on the nodding heads and backs of students who doodle when he is drawing perfect triangles and diagrams.

This time in Mr. Almeida's class, this kid Pablo pretends that he is this wrestler, Tito Santana. His body jitters and his feet can't keep still, and he suddenly jumps from desk to desk, yelling that he is the champion and not to take his belt. He grabs a pair of scissors, holds still and zig-zags around the room, like a fly, side to side.

This football game, that same year, starts with Pablo on the sidelines. He paces back and forth, like a chicken or a hen. He has stopped talking to anyone, coaches, players, friends. He runs out into the field and a flag goes into the wind. He gets taken out again, and then he wanders aimlessly around his team.

That one kid, Pablo, that one day at school, he tried that one ounce. That one ounce. That one kid.

Scene with Ricardo Montalbán: *Fantasy Island* (1977–1984)

My uncle tells me that Mr. Rourke didn't always wear a white suit.

He'd ride horses in corrals, chest to the screen, one time getting tossed into a wheelchair.

Leading actresses would wrap their wishes around his shoulders.

Now he sells dreams to men and women who carry their lives in their suitcases.

Some want heavier diamonds, others want to grow trees without having to water the roots.

Some seventh graders at my school have already started buying dreams that are offered with the shake of a hand and are sold in bathroom stalls.

They pay a few dollars for a few puffs and make straws out of bills.

My uncle can't stop tossing and turning.

He has dreams too.

I've read them in the money orders he sends to bill collectors and family members who beg for pills or the bite of a kernel of corn.

He took me in because he had borrowed from my _______ to get to New York. I'm a debt that can't be paid.

By the end of each episode, Mr. Rourke sends johns and alices back to the laundry basket routines of their lives.

Some don't make it out, but the ones who survive come back with new testaments dangling from the sides of their arms.

Each time I gulp water I keep my uncle away from his island.

As he places parts on conveyor belts during the day or flips burgers at night, I watch the islanders wait for their dreams to come true.

My uncle can't pay for drops of water with dirt from my fingernails.

And I can't stand by while his overworked fingernails curb into the shape of an empty spoon.

So at age 12, unable to get a job, I take my hands out of my pockets and start grabbing cans of food from groceries stores.

There is no man in a white suit to meet me and scold me for doing what I do. But this life he's living is no fantasy. And I do what I do in order to make his life come true.

Scene with Barbara Carrera: *Centennial* (1978–1979)

She is Mena. I know I've said it before. Lupe was Mena. But this is Mena now. Mena with long, dark hair. With cheekbones that call for more than kisses. Eyes that say smother me. She is wearing braids and talking to two white men loading their canoe. She is with her father and translates for him. He wants to know about their wives. One says he is married. When the other says that he is not, she smiles as the flute plays. Her eyes look down and can't hide her love for him. He says he will return. That man could be me in a canoe, paddling away and back to Mena. But women that look like her don't wind up with guys who look like me. It's only when they are little girls that they hold hands and hug you. Not even in movies. Not even when you have goods to trade. Instead, women like her stay in separate worlds, every now and then pretending to write letters. But even then, that too stops. At school, I can't find anyone who is like Mena. So until I do, I'll keep watching for her on TV, even if she is taken away and can't find me.

Scene from *State of Siege* (1972)

My uncle never has time to sit down for movies, but he has been telling me to let him know when this one airs.

He says he heard that it is about Latin American politics.

Dirty politics.

One guy at work tells him that it is a true story and that maybe, hey, maybe my uncle will be in the movie.

The night it airs, my uncle is wearing a T-shirt and jeans.

All the windows are open, but all that does is let the fires in.

He pours pineapple soda for us.

When the movie starts, he freezes, as if he has to study it for an exam.

"This movie isn't about our country," he says.

At first there is not much talking, just a lot of scenes with police and men wearing headsets and dragging rifles.

There is a blockade.

Men and cars are searched.

On a lonely street, a policeman drives up to a parked car.

The eyes of a blindfolded man in the backseat look toward the sky.

He is dead.

The characters speak in French at times, and their English is spoken with an accent that is difficult to follow.

The skin of the actors is fairer than anyone's in our family.

The adults all ride around in their own cars.

After yet another man is wrapped and carried inside a rug, I lose interest and refill my glass.

I wait for the film to end.

I wait for the police to stop chasing.

I wait for everyone to run out of bullets.

I wait for my uncle to stand up and walk away.

I wait for him to stop glaring ahead.

I wait for him to stop looking for himself.

I wait for him to say it again. "This movie isn't about our country."

Scene with Marcelino Sánchez: *The Warriors* (1979)

The first time I'm in a theater in the U.S., the Jesus
of gangsters fires shotgun chants at his Apostles
and stands at the peak of New York.

Colors fall unto his hands and each time he asks,
Canyoudigit? The audience answers with raised arms.

Rembrandt too.

The Warrior with woman's lips carries spray cans,
lets hunters know his gang lives. Tag saint defends
himself with paint. The Yankee Samurai bats miss
his head. As his brothers kiss the Sirens who carry
pool sticks, the little man says no to a dance and
warns his brothers about blades and guns. He
makes it to the clanks of Coney Island, long
enough for bottles to start rattling just before
coming out and play.

The first time I use spray paint, I'm with Jimmy
Henderson and Rolando Rodríguez. The store
clerk senses that our fingers are ready to pull
a trigger and picks out the colors. We carry
our ammunition in our backpacks. Jimmy
wants the first hit to be for revenge: the corner
market that fired his brother for not showing
up to work. Six times. Rolando wants us
to mark spots where the girls will see them.

We settle on a wall near the school, the side
of a building that sells midnight fires. Rolando
is the only one who has pulled a trigger
on a can before, so he starts us with the basics:
Twistthecap, andlineupthecannon. Shakethecan
overandover. Makesurethecanisvertical. And
runlikeheckifyouhearanysirensoranyscreams.

The wall is filled with a history of sunflower
love that has been erased and repainted as
park benches. That night we spray over
our endless mistakes and corrections:
cars turn into buses, clouds into oceans,
mountains into skyscrapers. Our full
moon into half a sun.

That wall becomes our gallery, new shows
every couple of weeks. We never paint
dried, sagging raisins. We color hollow stories
of beanstalks and cornstalks that touch
the top of Brooklyn Bridge. Cannons
in our hands, we kneel as we spray to our
God and exhale the dreams that movies
paint up and down alleys, on the sides
of crumbling walls and on the end
of streets that have been left for dead.

Scene from *El Norte* (1983)

My uncle tells me our family is made
of coffee beans. Like in the film.

The father of the farmed lands
gathers workers to unionize
but the union of force and blades
is a machete too strong for bones
of weeds. Soon, his head hangs
from a tree. A rope keeps it
midair, the sun about to shine
into what's left of his mouth.

Coffee, my uncles says, stains
the hands of picking—
inking the fingers that hold
cups of sip-
                pin',
keeping those memories from slip-
                                        pin'.

Our family used coffee beans to dye shirts
and bandanas, the grounds to feed
the sorghum, tamarind, papayas
and bananas (long before the crops
died of thirst). They picked beans
from birth of day to the drop
of legs
        and arms.

Apple crumbs on his lips,
my uncle takes that cup of sip-
                                    pin'.

As much as he tries to move
his eyes away from trees,
my uncle can't keep memories
from slip-
                pin'.

Coffee drip-
                pin',
his grayed head sags, like a sun
hanging from the universe, slip-
                                        pin'.

Scene with Elizabeth Peña: *El Super* (1979)

At the Rugby, the audience laughs so hard that I can hardly hear the lines. Elizabeth Peña fights with her family about life in the city.

About returning. About staying.
About *regresar*. About *quedar*.

El Super stomps on snow and kicks snowballs. He'd rather be in Miami's waters because even Miami is part of his Cuba.

His daughter refuses them, would rather smoke a joint than a Cuban cigar, would rather disco than mambo.

She prefers New York's streets.
Ella prefiere las calles de Nueva York.

The Super tells her to speak Spanish.
Ella le habla en inglés.

But I don't laugh. Not once.

There is too much of my uncle.
Mi tío.

There is too much of me.
De mí.

My uncle tells me to stop hanging out with my friends, that there is no point in being in New York if all I'm going to do is play with garbage.
Pero ¿qué basura?

When he finds a spray can under the sofa, he swears loudly and throws it in the garbage.

Pero ¿por qué en la basura?

Later that night, when the boys and I are out, I remember his anger, so I make sure to tag building walls in English and Spanish.

Pues, para mi tío.

Scene from *Walk Proud* (1979)

Robby Benson: we remember
his one on one dribbles. Baller
from a small town where cornstalks
replace corner street signs.

This time he is Emilio Méndez
with dark contact lenses, their
hardness poking his blue-eyed genes,
he brown make-up spray painted
on his face like the sign of a Crip.

To leave his gang of Aztecs,
he has to get jumped out,
walk down lines of street soldiers:
punches, fists, departing gifts
for this Latin King.

But for Rolando, Jimmy and me,
lying back on a sofa on a lazy
Sunday afternoon when even
the police don't bother to take
calls or circle around the block,
Benson's jump shots release
swarms of dreams and jokes.

Rolando says:
            That'ssoperverse,
            let'splayititinreverse.

And when we rewind the tape,
the punches become Emilio's
punishment for the claims to be
what he is not. He returns
his low rider, tosses out his

bandana, spits into beer cans
and goes back to Kansas.

We continue by playing our
own lives backwards:

Bus drivers give back nickels, sub-
ways rise off tracks, Jimmy's father
walks out of prison, his mother walks
out her boyfriend's bedroom. And my
neighbor, the old man on the sixth floor,
poses for a picture with family at his side,
his front door open wide, a baby in his arms,
his mouth swallowing his first slur.

Scene from *¿Qué Pasa, USA?* (1977–1980)

Sick of bathroom doors opening
and the morning rooster crowing,
Miami Joe runs away to a concrete block
with posters of rock stars, a peace
sign and a marijuana leaf on his wall.

It's his own private Cuba where
he can drink his own water and leave
his bed a mess. But when the secret of his
whereabouts gets released, his family comes
armed.

His grandmother carries the roach
spray, his mother the clean linens and his
father the toolbox. They want Miami Joe
to feel the breath of home in his escape
and are ready to fix his raft.

When Joe finds one of them hiding under
the table, another under the bed and the other
inside a closet, he apologizes for drifting,
and he returns home to the revelry of English
and Spanish and that rivalry between yelling
and screaming.

When Rolando and Jimmy come
to my uncle's apartment, no one is fighting
over what to watch on TV, no one is yelling
at the kitchen table.

They tell me I am lucky to have it all to myself. But when they leave, the silence bounces from wall to wall.

The only way to deafen it is to sit back and pretend I'm in Miami, in Joe's apartment, waiting for the Pérez family to come through the door and yell so loudly that even a fight feels like a touch of warm bread.

Scene from *Chips* (1977–1983)

Those Brooklyn cops prefer Pontiacs,
the 8-cylinders with the heavy doors,
speedometers with needles that touch
the towers. They don't bother with the L.A.
bikes that ride the highways, the boots
that choke the knees, the uniform
that hugs around their chests.

When Ponch catches teens riding
someone else's bike or skateboarding
down the wrong way lane, he flashes his
movie star smile and nudges them to do
the right thing. On Career Day, he
dresses the part and is back in school.
The young faces too much for him, he
chokes on his own stories.

He raps soft, like my uncle, who counts
the crumbs at our table and suspects
that loaves have come out of my pockets.

He tells me that if I ever have to wear
handcuffs, that he won't take time off
to greet me at the cell door:

It's your life and you can toss rocks at it
and dodge the stones that cops will hurl
at your feet, but I'm not the kind who uses
a belt to make your feet follow my beat.

He doesn't know I've come close twice.

The first time I almost get caught,
the owner of a deli sees me sneaking
a loaf of bread under my shirt and hurls
an empty soda can at my head. I run until
I'm locked at home. Police on TV
watch over me.

The second time I'm almost caught, I
am at a convenience store, hungry
for a dinner. I grab a can of tuna,
pretend that I'm tying my
shoes, and stuff it under my socks.
A boy from my school sees
me and calls me out.

Yo, yo.
Yo.
Yo, I'm talking to you.

I walk away without turning.

Yo, man.

Again, I run home and lock
the door, turn up the volume.

The next day at school, I'm
hanging in between history
and math, when that same
boy comes up from behind
and sucker punches me.
Books fall on the floor. My
ears ring, and I hear:

Don't you ever _____ come
near my__________ store. You
better __________ think twice
next time you __________, you
___________. You hear me.
My dad knows your ________.
And you're lucky I don't take
out my ________ to put a
__________ in your ________.
Next time , you'll have a
________________ inside your
_________________________.

I want to run but I have heavy stones on my feet. Faces around me. No cell, no cop to give me a speech. Just bruises, empty pockets and an empty stomach telling me there must be more.

Scene from *White Shadow* (1978–1981)

On Monday evenings, I catch up on homework while watching suicide drills. This time, Gómez isn't bouncing balls. He's catching Fs and writing about Zapata (*Little Women* aren't his thing). When the coach pulls his playing string, Gómez does what boys like him do on the screen. The Mexican flag sits on his belt, and gold hangs from his neck. He returns to bang with his old gang, the Aztecs (those same old suspects). They take the gold and silver by the handful, take stabs and bullets for each other. When the eye of one is taken by another, Gómez has to fight for his brother. But just as he is about to throw life in front of a train, his shadow rises to pull him from the mobs and to the corners of the courts, to disconnect the Xs from the Os, to keep the shots away from the sport. By the end of the show, Zapata has arrived at Carver High and Coach Reeves is rapping about black and brown. Gómez is in the hospital, but he'll be back on the team, ready to play again, ready to dream.

At my middle school, the shadows don't follow us. Instead, we chase the shadows into darkness. We can see better that way, away from the strobe lights and far from the flashes and ashes that rest on our lashes, blinding us so badly that we have no choice but to close our eyes. I don't ball. Never could. I trip over hard wood, and besides, I don't trust the rust on baskets. I'm no athlete. And in the classroom, I don't catch Fs, but I don't shoot As or Bs either. The boys with detentions and no retention, they are the ones who get the attention. But not me. No way. I slide slick into the back row and keep my head up while teachers lay up formulas and words. Once in a while, the answers fall on my hands, but not so much that teachers' shadows follow me. That's okay. Because in my dreams, it's so dark that when Zapata visits, no one can flash pictures of his dead body or catch his shadow. In my dreams, Zapata is living off the darkness that the world has given him.

Scene with Barbara Carrera: *Never Say Never Again* (1983)

They made her the Bond girl.
She is a Bond girl.
She bonded with James.
She made it to Bond.
He made her his girl.
Bond's girl.
The girl for Bond.
She became the one.
She water-skied into his arms.
She was wearing a bathing suit.
He opened his arms in his vanilla suit.
He held a martini at his side.

I wish I could be the one who held her in his arms.
But it's like at school, I'm not the one.

The girls would rather be with the guys
who are like Bond.

She was the Indian girl with black braids.
Now she is a Bond girl.
A gone girl.

Scene from *Boulevard Nights* (1979)

Knives.

Chuco believes in them
and their afterlife.

After the workday ends,
the blade keeps Chuco from
walking away.

His tattoo is a birthmark
of his rebirth of thirst.

He uses spray cans to fly high.

He starts believing in magnums,
starts chasing low-riders,
starts dancing with his back
toward windows, his feet
facing sharp edges.

Gangs.

Jimmy, Rolando and I
shouldn't believe in them.

Should know that the screens
are rabbit holes leading
to fantasies of wonderlands.

But we've also seen gang
letters covering up our tags
on walls.

We've seen the colors
on shirts at school, the colors
on the jackets, the colors
on the hats, the graffiti
over ours.

And now even cousins'
cousins are wearing
the bandanas.

The ones who don't
are the ones who put
up fists last and use
their hands to catch
their fall.

So we form our own.

First. We pick
names. Warriors,
taken. Delinquents,
taken. Mafia,
taken. Block Boys,
taken. Brown Lords,
taken. Wolf Pack,
taken. Young Bosses,
taken. Boulevard Boys.
Like the movie.
We take it.

Second. We pick colors.
Navy blue. Taken.
Blood red. Taken.
Army green. Taken.

Sky gray. Taken.
We settle on white
shirts. Blue pants.

At school. Not one
teacher, custodian,
principal, student,
secretary, dean,
parent, aide,
cafeteria worker
cares. Not one
says a thing.

At home. Rolando's
ma, Jimmy's
dad, my
uncle, don't
notice
the swaggers
of our
tank
tops.

We try to make
them turn
their heads.

We use our spray
cannons, unload
them
up and
down
Brooklyn buildings.

We tag our
Name:
Boulevard
Boys. BB.

The rest
of Brooklyn
may not
notice, but spray
cans give breath
to our gang
of three
and keep us
from
believing
in blades,
guns and
knives.

No one knows it.

But
paint
keeps
cuts,
bullets,
wounds,
out of our
lives.

Scene with Edward James Olmos: *Zoot Suit* (1981)

His pachuco talk,
his pachuco walk,
his pachuco swagger.

He is on the side
of the heroes
and the fools.

The black zoot suit,
the red shirt with wide collars,
the crucifix hanging below his heart.

He is the right
and the wrong
of Henry Reyna.

Snaps the fingers
and plays the piano
to the tune of laughter.

He is a shadow from the streets
or a black light darkening
a crack on the moon.

He knows Sleepy Lagoon,
what lies in the deep,
waiting to be awakened.

He brings nickels
to the court trial,
the carnival with restless rides.

And by the end,
he is cornered
by acrobats who spit fire.

He curls
himself
into a fetal position.

And bellows
his naked,
native cry.

We are 14, laughing
in Ms. Bari's class
when we first hear it.

We are 14, crying
in the streets when we
see the first chalk outline.

Scene from *The Ballad of Gregorio Cortez* (1982)

A sheriff. Looking for a man who traded
a horse. A translator. Tells about a man who
supposedly denies trading a horse, who
supposedly refuses to admit a crime, who
supposedly says no man can arrest him.

A sheriff's death. Translated as a murder.

When my clothes sat in suitcases, my uncle
would translate the aches from my stomach
to the corner pharmacist. My haircuts to
barbers. After the scissors and the pills, my
hair would sometimes be just as long, and
my stomach would still gurgle its pain.

Now that my clothes are two sizes bigger,
he is the one who tosses Spanish words
to me so that I can catch them, turn them
into English and pass them to someone
else. I treat them as if they had shells
around them. The time he had me meet
with his boss who had docked him
for having the flu, I dropped the words
on tile and he almost got fired.

Gregorio Cortez was an outlaw. The pistol
in his hand less dangerous than the Spanish
in his mouth. At night I take a dictionary
the size of a brick and use it to load my
English. No horses, sheriffs or wagons
on our roads. But the more words I carry,
the more dangerous my trigger becomes.

Scene from *Scarface* (1983)

Rolando's dad is gone.

Jimmy says heshouldbeoutbythetimeRolandograduatesfromhigh school.

We don't ask.

Not even about the rumors that dollars were hidden inside stuffed animals.

Newspapers report his sins.

Neighbors whisper his guilt.

My uncle tells me I should've known anyway.

> *Didn't I see how Rolando's family always*
> *bought the most expensive birthday gifts for any party?*
> *Plus the father only worked as a contractor and never*
> *carried a hammer?*

Jimmy and I don't ask Rolando about any of it.

But a few months later, Tony Montana enters the screen, and his scar stretches so far that it starts to reach into our neighborhood.

We can't go half a block without hearing someone yell out Sayhellotomylittlefriend.

At school, the black and white T-shirts surround us.

Al Pacino stares straight ahead, holding a gun at his side.

A cigar with puffs of smoke slithers its way into the cafeteria.

Students yell out,
When you get the money,
you get the power, then
you get the women.

High-fives fly above classroom clocks.

Powder fills the air almost as much as dust.

In the meantime, Rolando keeps quiet.

Like he doesn't hear the cocaine hollers of bags of dollars.

By the end of the year, he and his family pack their mattresses into the back of a station wagon without telling anyone where they'll stop.

He doesn't call, doesn't write to either of us.

Jimmy says
Theytookoffbecause
theystillhaveallthatmoney
andtheydon'twantanyone
tochasehimdown.

But I think they just want a new town, a new state, a new school, a new start.

Without Rolando's fingerprints, we have to cap our spray cans. It's not the same without his edges.

He was the one with notebooks full of sketches.

Gangs and lovers paint over what used to be ours.

Murals have no memories of their beginnings or ends.

In Brooklyn, the name Rolando is fading away.

But we all remember his father.

His name, when he had the money, when he pretended any of us could have the power.

Scene with Esai Morales: *Bad Boys* (1983)

Revenge: Moreno rapes for it. Takes off
his mask for it. Goes to prison for it. He
swallows drops of his own blood to get
a taste of someone else's blood for it.
He is the savage with a spear who must
fight for it. He is not the little, charming
boy with exploding wires and mouse traps
backing into it. He is not the little boy
with the smug lips who trips over it. He
is not O'Brien, the one who kills brothers
by accident and runs far away from it. He
is not the one who can turn his back to it.

The bad boys, they hang on crosses
at the end of movies. Some are named
O'Brien and are forgiven for they know
not what they do. Others are named
Moreno. Their own names won't let them
escape from themselves. We know what
they do. They do what they know. They
seek revenge and know what to do.

They say that they grew full of primitive
rage. That they are raised in cities
without altars, and maybe they are born
to families without fathers. Maybe they steal
and kill on the blocks, they get locked down,
they stock up on revenge and would
rather die alone than live with enemies.

I have a social studies teacher who doesn't
teach. He sits in front with his legs crossed
while the rest of us hang and talk. He asks us
about the latest rumors, who'sbeenarrested,

who'sgettinglockedup? I doubt his fingers have
ever touched chalk. He calls us his Bad Boys
and has this whocares, I'mstillgettingpaid kind
of laugh. He gives us all Bs for letting him be.

The grades he gives are bribes telling us to keep
looking toward the sky. That's why no one
complains. But I'm a Bad Boy, made that
way, my teacher says, just like my last name.
And it's true, I used to whistle about love,
about hands locked under moons and suns
rising above oceans. But love has failed me.

I carry a pencil without an eraser, and I use it
to draw memories, like the one of Mr. _____
joking with the class about the Bad Boys
who went away and used to be my boys.
He can't hear my I'llstillgetmyrevenge
kind of laugh, or the sound of my pencil's
crack, or the blocks tumbling when I rise
from my desk in the back.

As I approach him one-on-one after class,
my stomp resurrects the names of Bad Boys:
Rodríguez
Martínez
Ramírez
Pérez
Left
Right
Left
Right

Rodríguez
            Martínez
                        Ramírez
                                    Pérez
                                                Left
Right
            Left
Right.

For them, for me, I'll refuse his B. Their memories, their names, is all I have left.

Scene from *My Family/Mi Familia* (1995)

He has married her (for papers).

Because the nun (who is his sister) insisted that he save the woman (from El Salvador).

Because the sister who used to be a nun had nowhere else to turn.

(Because the woman from El Salvador had nowhere else to run.)

He says I do and then tries to run away (but the sister grabs his arm and corners him to the back of the room).

Yes, he says.

They marry (because he is the brother who wants to help the sister helping the woman who left El Salvador).

But he resists her smile (and her curves).

Until one day when the music (mambo) pulls him toward her.

That night the L.A. lights shine on them (as they make love).

After the sweat, he holds her tightly (and tells her about his brother).

(The night of the owl.)

She tells him about her family (her father).

(The massacres.)

The truth is that Mena never wrote a letter (to me).

She has probably forgotten me (or the taste of the candy).

I used to think that maybe the two of us would reunite in the U.S. (recognizing ourselves by the light in our eyes).

The truth is I didn't expect to see her today (but there she is, crying on the big screen about the death squads).

And here I am, no longer crying about what could have been.

(But crying about what may have been).

AFTERWORD: LAST CUT

Scenes from '80s Reels

My boulevard brothers were no longer next to me after the low of high
school. That first summer, I got a job landscaping, mostly mowing

grass at city parks. The workers had more stubble in their faces than I did,
but they were young enough to rap TV, old enough for widescreen scenes

and rename me. I wore a bandana to work one day, and as I was picking
up weeds, someone planted a seed. He called me Cheech. I tried fighting

back and started making spoons out of deadwood. I tried to start a fire with
sticks and exhale the gasoline from inside me, but nothing would light.

I fought the nickname with cactus needless and asked for water from
my first Baptism, but they laughed and wouldn't cut the clips. Cheech

I would be. I told them to call me by the name my mother and father
had bled for but they wouldn't listen. My mouth tried to do tricks

to make sure the name wouldn't stick, but their tongues released Cheech,
that was it. I waited for time to rename me, but the clocks wouldn't tick.

I became what they called me, and every now and then, we'd get
high on rockets and pretend to plant a flag on a new moon. We

would sit back and break the afternoon into pieces, complain about long
hours, low pay and wait for the evening trains to release us. Most

workers were into the Jets and the Mets, but more than anything, they
wanted their MTV. How they loved the silver gloves, the takes on me.

They chimed on about how that ain't working, how the videos were killing
the radio stars. One afternoon, we were near the clouds, clipping branches

when one of the guys laughed about a video in which a guy with greasy hair and a greasy gold chain tries to pick up a woman who is buying mints.

She steps back and turns him down, yelling, *not if you was the last immigrant grocer on earth, honey*. Not even. The workers laughed as leaves fell.

A week later, as I was taking a ladder to a tree and asked for someone to hold it, one of them repeated it. *notifyouwasthelast immigrantgroceronearth, honey*.

I could have snapped the rungs, but I knew freezing my lips was a better way to be a part of this crew, even if it meant taking the punch line in the ribs.

When the grass stopped growing and the cold cut the leaves from trees, we said our goodbyes and I went to work stocking food at a corner

grocery store. My job was to square up the cans and food boxes so that the logos faced the shoppers, Chef Boyardee grinning and greeting

them at every turn. Old habits weren't easy to break. During breaks, I'd eat the apples that I'd slip into my pocket. As I lined up goods

in marching formation, I'd hear the voices behind the aisles: babies crying to get fed, mothers looking for sale items, single men asking

for frozen foods, teens searching for chocolate bars. The regulars were easy to recognize. Something about their eyes, like they were

taking food out of their own cupboards. There was this family of four, mother's hair was always flustered, baby usually had a runny nose.

She used to buy bananas by the bunches. As she drove her cart up and down lanes to make her baby smile, she would do a little

sway with her hips, then sing about Chiquita bananas, strong accent on top of her head. It seemed like every week she would go out

of her way to chop up her pronunciations. I started hearing the accent
all around me. At night, when I watched the rerun channel, I saw

José Jiménez say his name. Each joke the same, he gave lessons on how to
say jo jo jo, then he told Milton Berle that he was from Halabama,

with a Banho on his knee. When the moon came out from hiding,
I'd watch the same characters dressed with the same accent. I saw

Ramiro González-González's Engleesh make Groucho's eyebrows spin.
During the day, I carried my accent back and forth telling shoppers where

to find the condees, the spechials, the frossen mels. Every time I spoke, I
waited for the laugh tracks, kept looking back to check on customers' faces

to spot a grin. It didn't matter if their lips curved up or if they just kept moving
along. The echoes of laughter would ring in my mind. I began to slice and dice

my sentences in half, spitting a simple number when people looked at me
and asked, where is this, where is that? I worked at that store nearly mute

for nearly a year. I chopped off all my English words and their roots. I would
work and watch TV, my own accent mocking me. The tongue that cut

my skin was beginning to cut off my breathing. The few times I spoke,
words sounded like desperate wheezing. I'd start to relax, try to forget laugh

tracks, watch the terrestrial before he got home, hear Chewbacca groan, see
Indiana Jones almost face doom. But the accent was like this roaming mutt

that wouldn't get lost. I was stuck in the same scene, and when Chrissy
left Jack and Janet, and Felipe came in, the laugh tracks came back,

yet again. My tongue went into hiding, held its own strike. I tried to use it,
but all it could say was ____________. The world was_________. The moon

was ________. The sun was ________. I would live in the __________. I
watched more of what I became. I rented films with silent black and silent

white and watched Myrtle González carry buckets, serve coffee, stack wood. I saw
flowers in the air, white horses gallop with pride, Ramón Novarro, arms akimbo,

as Ben-Hur. Silence bred more silence, and the more of these films I watched,
the louder the loneliness of my uncle's apartment became. My eardrums hurt

like they were going to burst. But I had to keep the reel rolling. I went so far
back that I found faces from my childhood, Dolores del Río, Lupe Vélez.

The men in the films were lovers, headlining kisses. Then something strange
happened to the strips. The stubble started to grow on the dark faces.

Titles started to grow the word greaser. Latin lovers became dirty fighters,
latin mermaids became housemaids. The more of them started to clean

and fill the screen, the more I wanted to hear their voices. I tried turning it
up as high as I could but nothing came. Their whispers were silenced

and so were their screams. I was stuck in a cycle, silent work and silent films.
Every time my uncle came around, he'd look at me and shake his head.

He'd yell at me to go outside, to go touch the sky. I was sure no one would
hear my accent in public again. I was stuck in two scenes and would have

gone back and forth forever if not for one day when I was doing my usual
squaring and my usual muting, pointing to aisles one, two, three.

I had already put a forbidden apple in my pocket and was shuffling my
feet toward the exit doors, when the manager, this tall guy with

bifocals and this wide company tie, followed me until his breath on my
back made me stop. I was half a step from the sliding glass doors.

He tapped me on my shoulder. I didn't even turn toward him. I had worked there for fourteen months, but he didn't even know my name.

He just touched my arm and said, excusemeyoungman,weneed totalk. I took the apple out of my pocket, handed it to him and walked and

walked past all of Brooklyn. He didn't come after me. For all I know, he is still standing there, apple in hand. I didn't take the subway home

that day. I walked past my past. Past the school where a boy named Jimmy introduced himself to me, index finger resting on a spray can.

The streets where Rolando tagged our names in 3D. The Beverly Theater where the three of us ran to see Cyrus get shot. As I passed

the video store that raised me, I couldn't help but rent a film for time's sake. It took me almost two hours to get to my street,

and another half hour to drag my feet up to the altar of my uncle's TV. I put the tape into the player and stared at the opening scene:

a dark-haired, young boy with almond eyes frozen still. He has rough, dark skin that looks like it has been toughened by a northern sun.

He is in handcuffs. He closes his eyes, and a woman comes to his side. She moves like Mena and looks like she wants to glide her fingers

through his hair. I wait for some hero to arrive and start a war, save and then take the girl, then aim, ready, fire at the prisoner. But instead,

the boy is left alone. There is no music. No sound. He opens his mouth wide, like he is screaming and trying to force out what's inside. I edge

forward and get so close that the screen begins to fog up. And then I get so close that I can hear the boy's screams. I get so close that I begin

to save him by turning away from him and turning inside the pages of books and inside the dreams that are hidden inside the love of me.

Biography

José B. González is the author of *Toys Made of Rock.* He was born in San Salvador, El Salvador, and lived there until the age of eight; at which point, he emigrated to the United States and was reunited with his parents, who had left to escape their country's civil turmoil and to find work.

A Fulbright Scholar to Spain, he has been the recipient of such honors as the New England Association of Teachers of English Poet of the Year Award and the American Association of Hispanics in Higher Education Outstanding Latino Faculty of the Year Award. His work has been anthologized in the *Norton Introduction to Literature, Theatre Under My Skin: Contemporary Salvadoran Poetry, The Wandering Song: Central American Writing in the United States,* and journals such as *Callaloo*, *Calabash* and *Palabra*. A member of the Macondo Writers Workshop, he is the co-editor, with John S. Christie, of *Latino Boom: An Anthology of U.S. Latino Literature*.

A nationally known speaker, González has presented at various colleges, such as: Harvard University and Cornell University; countries including Mexico, Spain and El Salvador; and institutions including the Smithsonian Latino Center and the Smithsonian Museum of the American Indian. The founder and editor of LatinoStories.com, he has been featured in the nationally syndicated show American Latino TV and has been a contributor to National Public Radio.

Once a non-English speaker, he now has a Ph.D. in English and is a Professor of English at the U.S. Coast Guard Academy in New London, CT. He lives in Quaker Hill, CT with his wife, three strong daughters and a son who is starting to believe that being a strong man and standing up for women's rights can go hand in hand.